~A BINGO BOOK~

Vermont Bingo Book

COMPLETE BINGO GAME IN A BOOK

Written By Rebecca Stark

ISBN 978-0-87386-538-8

Educational Books 'n' Bingo

Printed in the U.S.A.

DIRECTIONS

INCLUDED:

List of Terms

Templates for Additional Terms and Clues

2 Clues per Term

30 Unique Bingo Cards

Markers

1. **Either cut apart the book or make copies of ALL the sheets. You might want to make an extra copy of the clue sheets to use for introduction and review. Keep the sheets in an envelope for easy reuse.**

2. Cut apart the call cards with terms and clues.

3. Pass out one bingo card per student. There are enough for a class of 30.

4. Pass out markers. You may cut apart the markers included in this book or use any other small items of your choice.

5. Decide whether or not you will require the entire card to be filled. Requiring the entire card to be filled provides a better review. However, if you have a short time to fill, you may prefer to have them do the just the border or some other format. Tell the class before you begin what is required.

6. There are 50 terms. Read the list before you begin. If there are any terms that have not been covered in class, you may want to read to the students the term and clues before you begin.

7. There is a blank space in the middle of each card. You can instruct the students to use it as a free space or you can write in answers to cover terms not included. Of course, in this case you would create your own clues. (Templates provided.)

8. Shuffle the cards and place them in a pile. Two or three clues are provided for each term. If you plan to play the game with the same group more than once, you might want to choose a different clue for each game. If not, you may choose to use more than one clue.

9. Be sure to keep the cards you have used for the present game in a separate pile. When a student calls, "Bingo," he or she will have to verify that the correct answers are on his or her card AND that the markers were placed in response to the proper questions. Pull out the cards that are on the student's card keeping them in the order they were used in the game. Read each clue as it was given and ask the student to identify the correct answer from his or her card.

10. If the student has the correct answers on the card AND has shown that they were marked in response to the *correct questions,* then that student is the winner and the game is over. If the student does not have the correct answers on the card OR he or she marked the answers in response to *the wrong questions,* then the game continues until there is a proper winner.

11. If you want to play again, reshuffle the cards and begin again.

Have fun!

TERMS INCLUDED

Agricultural

Ethan Allan

Apple(s)

Chester Alan Arthur

Battle of Bennington

Border (-ed)

Burlington

Samuel de Champlain

Champlain Valley

Climate

Camel's Hump Mountain

Constitution

Calvin Coolidge

County (-ies)

Covered Bridge(s)

Executive Branch

Fish

Flag

France

French and Indian War

Grossular Garnet

Green Mountain(s)

Hermit Thrush

Insect(s)

Judicial Branch

Lake Champlain

Legislative Branch

Manufacture

Maple

Montpelier

Mount Mansfield

New Hampshire Grants

Northern Leopard Frog

New England

Northeast Highlands

Painted Turtle

Red Clover

Rutland

River(s)

Rocks

Seal

Ski (-ing)

Taconic Mountains

Talc

"These Green Mountains"

Tribes

Union

Vermont Republic

Vermont Piedmont

Vermont Valley

Vermont Bingo

Additional Terms

Choose as many additional terms as you would like and write them in the squares. Repeat each as desired.
Cut out the squares and randomly distribute them to the class.
Instruct the students to place their square on the center space of their card.

Vermont Bingo

Clues for Additional Terms

Write two clues for each of your additional terms.

1. 2.	1. 2.
1. 2.	1. 2. .
1. 2.	1. 2.

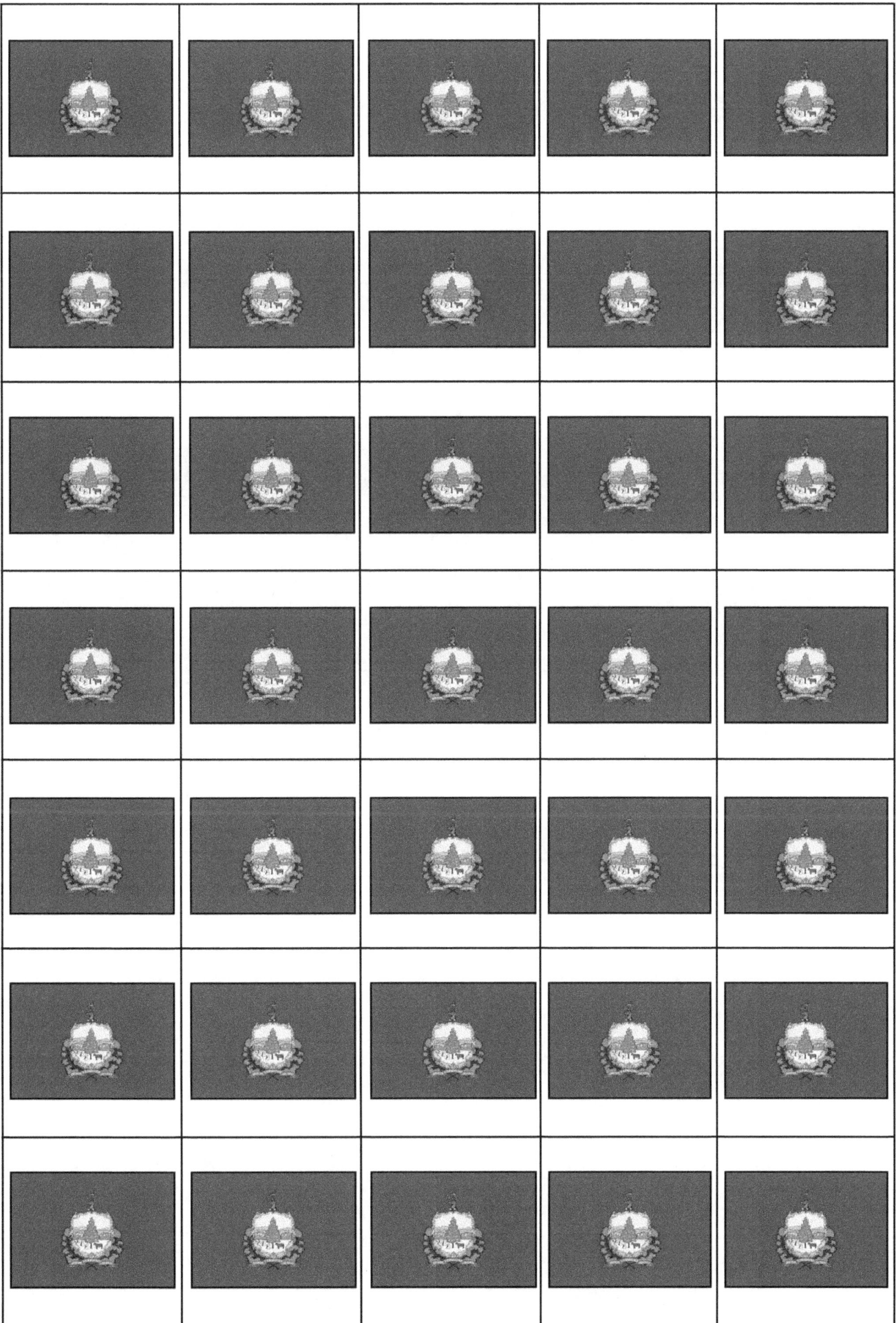

Agricultural 1. Important ___ products are dairy products, beef cattle and calves, greenhouse and nursery products, hay, and maple products. 2. About 3/4 of the state's ___ income comes from the sale of dairy products.	**Ethan Allan** 1. ___ was leader of the Green Mountain Boys. 2. With Benedict Arnold, ___ and his Green Mountain Boys captured Fort Ticonderoga from the British in 1775.
Apple(s) 1. The ___ is the state fruit. ___ pie is the state pie. 2. ___ are the largest fruit crop.	**Chester Alan Arthur** 1. ___, the 21st President, was born in Vermont. The re-creation of the house in which he lived as an infant is a state historic site. 2. ___ became President after the assassination of President Garfield.
Battle of Bennington] 1. The ___ took place on August 18, 1777. The British defeat led to the surrender of General Burgoyne at Saratoga, said to be the turning point of the Revolutionary War. 2. The anniversary of this battle is a legal holiday in Vermont.	**Border (-ed)** 1. Three states ___ Vermont: Massachusetts, New Hampshire, and New York. 2. Vermont is ___ by Canada on the north.
Burlington 1. ___ is the largest city in Vermont. 2. ___ is located on the eastern shore of Lake Champlain.	**Samuel de Champlain** 1. This French explorer and navigator mapped much of northeastern North America. 2. In 1609 ___ mapped and described the great lake on the border of Vermont and New York. That lake is named for him.
Champlain Valley 1. ___ is also called the Vermont Lowland. 2. ___ is fertile farmland. Burlington is in this region.	**Climate** 1. Vermont's ___ is continental moist. Summers are warm to cool, and winters are cold. 2. Vermont's ___ is characterized by mild summers and cold winters. Vermont has four distinct seasons.

Vermont Bingo

Camel's Hump Mountain 1. ___ is one of the highest mountains in Vermont. It is on the state quarter. 2. ___ is so named because its two "humps" resemble those of a Bactrian camel.	**Constitution** 1. The ___ of the Vermont Republic was the first in America to prohibit slavery, the first to allow men to vote without property ownership, and the first to authorize a public school system. 2. The ___ of the Vermont Republic was adopted in Windsor in 1777. The Old ___ House in Windsor is now a state historic site.
Calvin Coolidge 1. President ___ was born in Plymouth Notch. The ___ Homestead District is a state historical site. 2. ___ became the 30th President when President Harding died. He was sworn in as President by his father in his boyhood home.	**County (-ies)** 1. Vermont has 14 ___. In Vermont, a ___ seat is called a shire town. 2. The largest Vermont ___ by population is Chittenden; the largest by size is Windsor.
Covered Bridge(s) 1. At one time there were more than 600 ___ in Vermont. Today there are about 100. 2. The Vermont ___ Museum is in Bennington. It is near 5 authentic ___.* *They are Silk Bridge, Henry Bridge, West Arlington Bridge, Paper Mill Village Bridge, and Chiselville Bridge.	**Executive Branch** 1. The ___ of government enacts and enforces the laws. It comprises the governor, the lt. governor, the secretary of state, the state treasurer, the auditor of accounts, the attorney general, and several agencies. 2. The governor is head of the ___. The present-day governor is [fill in].
Fish 1. The state cold-water ___ is the brook trout. 2. The state warm-water ___ is the Walleye pike.	**Flag** 1. The state ___ features the state coat of arms against a field of blue. 2. The state seal and the state ___ both contain the motto "Freedom and Unity."
France 1. During its early colonial period, the territory that is now Vermont was part of New ___. 2. In 1609 French explorer Samuel de Champlain claimed Vermont as part of New ___. Vermont Bingo	**French and Indian War** 1. The ___ was fought between the British and the French and their Native American allies. 2. The Treaty of Paris of 1763 ended the ___. As a result of this treaty France ceded the lands of New France to Great Britain.

Green Mountain(s) 1. Vermont is known as the ___ State. 2. When Samuel de Champlain saw the ___ in 1647, he called them *"Verts Monts."*	**Grossular Garnet** 1. ___ is the state gem. 2. Belvidere Mine at Eden Mills produces fine specimens of ___, the state gem.
Hermit Thrush 1. The ___ is the state bird. 2. The ___ was chosen as the state bird because of its pleasant call and the fact that it is found in all 14 counties.	**Insect(s)** 1. Two ___ are official state symbols: the honeybee and the Monarch butterfly. 2. The honeybee is the state ___. It is an official symbol in 17 states, probably because it plays such an important role in agriculture.
Judicial Branch 1. The ___ interprets what our laws mean and makes decisions about the laws and those who break them. 2. The Supreme Court is the highest court in the ___ of the state government.	**Lake Champlain** 1. ___ forms half of Vermont's western border, which it shares with the state of New York. 2. ___ is in the valley between the Green Mountains of Vermont and the Adirondack Mountains of New York. Its jutting shoreline is known as Chimney Point.
Legislative Branch 1. The ___ of government comprises the Senate and the House of Representatives. 2. The ___ makes the laws.	**Manufacture** 1. The ___ of electrical equipment is an important industry. 2. The production of food products and the ___ of machinery are also important industries.
Maple 1. The sugar ___ is the state tree. 2. Vermont is the leading producer of ___ syrup in the United States.	**Montpelier** 1. ___ is the capital of Vermont. 2. ___ is the least populous state capital in the nation.
Vermont Bingo	© Barbara M. Peller

Mount Mansfield 1. At 4,393 feet, ___ is the highest point in the state. 2. ___ and Camel's Hump are in the Green Mountains.	**New Hampshire Grants** 1. The ___ were land grants made between 1749 and 1764 by the provincial governor of New Hampshire. The land was also claimed by the Province of New York. 2. Bennington, chartered on January 3, 1749, was the first of the ___.
Northern Leopard Frog 1. The ___ is the state amphibian. 2. This amphibian helps control the number of insects and pests in the state's ponds. It helps keep the wetlands clean by eating algae.	**New England** 1. ___ comprises Maine, New Hampshire, Vermont, Massachusetts, Rhode Island, and Connecticut. 2. Vermont is the only ___ state without an ocean border.
Northeast Highlands 1. The ___ covers the northeast corner of the state. 2. The ___ is characterized by granite mountains, including Gore Mountain, Burke Mountain, and Mt. Monadnock. They are separated by swiftly flowing streams.	**Painted Turtle** 1. The ___ is the state reptile. 2. This reptile, which can withstand cold temperatures, is common in Vermont.
Red Clover 1. The ___ is state flower. 2. The ___ was designated the state flower because it is "symbolic of Vermont's scenic countryside… and of its dairy farms."	**Rutland** 1. ___ is in an area often called the "Crossroads of Vermont." The Norman Rockwell Museum of Vermont is in this city. 2. The Vermont State Fair is held annually in ___ at the Vermont State Fairgrounds.
River(s) 1. Connecticut, West, Otter, and Winooski are important ___ in the state. 2. The Vermont Piedmont is covered by the fertile lowlands of the Connecticut ___ Valley.	**Rocks** 1. Granite, marble, and slate are the official state ___. 2. Granite, one of the official state ___, is the most important mined product in the state.

Vermont Bingo

Seal
1. The wooded hills on the Great ___ indicate the Green Mountains.
2. The sheaves of wheat and the cow on the Great ___ symbolize agriculture.

Ski (-ing)
1. ___ and snowboarding are the official state winter sports.
2. Many tourists come to Vermont in the winter because of its ___ fine resorts.*

*These resorts include Stowe, Killington, Mt. Snow, Okemo, Jay Peak, Sugarbush, and Smugglers Notch.

Taconic Mountains
1. The ___ extend from Massachusetts and cover a a narrow strip in the southwestern part of Vermont. The area is characterized by mountains, swift streams, and beautiful lakes.
2. Equinox Mountain, Dorset Peak, Little Equinox Mountain, Mother Myrick Mountain, and Bear Mountain are in the ___.

Talc
1. ___ is the state mineral.
2. ___ is a soft, pale green mineral found in southwestern Vermont.

"These Green Mountains"
1. ___ is the state song.
2. The first line in ___ is "These green hills and silver waters."

Tribes
1. Prior to the arrival of Europeans, the Abenaki, the Mohican, and the Pennacook ___ lived in Vermont.
2. Today there are no federally recognized Native American ___ in Vermont. They are not extinct, but they do not live in the state.

Union
1. Vermont was admitted to the ___ on March 4, 1791.
2. When Vermont joined the ___ as the 14th state, it was the first outside the original colonies.

Vermont Republic
1. The ___ existed from 1777 to 1791.
2. For the first six months of its existence, the ___ was called The Republic of New Connecticut.

Vermont Piedmont
1. The ___, which is east of the Green Mountains, is also called the Western New England Upland.
2. The ___ includes most of Vermont's Connecticut River Valley; it is the largest physiographic region in the state.

Vermont Valley
1. The ___ is a small strip of land between the Taconic Mountains on the west and the Green Mountains on the east. It is considered an extension of the Vermont Lowlands.
2. The Baton Kill and Waloomsac rivers are found in this narrow valley region.

Vermont Bingo

Rutland	Agricultural	Apple(s)	France	Battle of Bennington
Fish	Ethan Allan	Vermont Piedmont	Grossular Garnet	Seal
Vermont Republic	Montpelier		Northeast Highlands	Vermont Valley
Union	Rocks	Tribes	Maple	New Hampshire Grants
New England	Hermit Thrush	County (-ies)	Talc	Lake Champlain

Vermont Bingo: Card No. 1

Vermont
Bingo

Harold or Sanctuary	France	Appeler	Jacquelin	Holland
Seal	Brosseau Clarel	Vermont plowman	Ethan Allen	Plath
Vermont Valley	Northeast Highlands		Montpelier	Vermont Republic
New Hampshire Granite	Maple	Trees	Barton	Bunion
Lake Champlain	Tate	Ocupy (-ies)	Hermit Thrush	New England

Vermont Bingo

Union	Vermont Republic	Judicial Branch	River(s)	Manufacture
New Hampshire Grants	Covered Bridge(s)	Samuel de Champlain	Rocks	Northern Leopard Frog
Climate	Hermit Thrush		Insect(s)	Tribes
Painted Turtle	Red Clover	Montpelier	Ski (-ing)	Battle of Bennington
Seal	Vermont Piedmont	County (-ies)	Fish	Talc

Vermont Bingo: Card No. 2

Vermont Bingo

Hermit Thrush	Tribes	Covered Bridge(s)	Maple	Vermont Republic
New Hampshire Grants	Ethan Allan	Champlain Valley	Agricultural	Green Mountain(s)
Rocks	Vermont Piedmont		Northern Leopard Frog	Chester Alan Arthur
Montpelier	Climate	New England	Painted Turtle	Judicial Branch
Talc	Camel's Hump Mountain	County (-ies)	Ski (-ing)	Manufacture

Vermont Bingo

Montpelier	Northern Leopard Frog	Apple(s)	Camel's Hump Mountain	Manufacture
Mount Mansfield	Burlington	Agricultural	River(s)	Vermont Republic
Northeast Highlands	Painted Turtle		Lake Champlain	France
Tribes	Ethan Allan	Vermont Piedmont	County (-ies)	Samuel de Champlain
Constitution	Seal	Border (-ed)	Talc	Vermont Valley

Vermont Bingo: Card No. 4

Vermont Bingo

Seal	Battle of Bennington	Rocks	Samuel de Champlain	Camel's Hump Mountain
Mount Mansfield	Tribes	Champlain Valley	Insect(s)	Ethan Allan
Apple(s)	Vermont Valley		Grossular Garnet	French and Indian War
Lake Champlain	Manufacture	Rutland	Ski (-ing)	Calvin Coolidge
Covered Bridge(s)	County (-ies)	Vermont Republic	Montpelier	Northeast Highlands

Vermont Bingo: Card No. 5

Vermont Bingo

Chester Alan Arthur	Northern Leopard Frog	Judicial Branch	Manufacture	Vermont Valley
Maple	Rocks	Calvin Coolidge	Agricultural	Vermont Republic
River(s)	Constitution		Burlington	Insect(s)
County (-ies)	New England	Ski (-ing)	Border (-ed)	Apple(s)
New Hampshire Grants	Samuel de Champlain	Rutland	Northeast Highlands	Executive Branch

Vermont Bingo

Rutland	Northern Leopard Frog	French and Indian War	Tribes	Covered Bridge(s)
New Hampshire Grants	Manufacture	Hermit Thrush	Ethan Allan	Mount Mansfield
Vermont Valley	France		Insect(s)	Burlington
Montpelier	Painted Turtle	Champlain Valley	Union	Climate
County (-ies)	Camel's Hump Mountain	Ski (-ing)	Border (-ed)	Chester Alan Arthur

Vermont Bingo

Northeast Highlands	Northern Leopard Frog	Flag	Maple	Burlington
Mount Mansfield	Apple(s)	River(s)	Vermont Valley	Samuel de Champlain
Executive Branch	Camel's Hump Mountain		Manufacture	Battle of Bennington
Talc	Montpelier	Union	Constitution	Painted Turtle
Vermont Piedmont	County (-ies)	Border (-ed)	Rocks	New Hampshire Grants

Vermont Bingo

Insect(s)	Covered Bridge(s)	Hermit Thrush	Executive Branch	Camel's Hump Mountain
Constitution	Manufacture	Northeast Highlands	Rocks	Northern Leopard Frog
Green Mountain(s)	Rutland		Ethan Allan	Flag
Calvin Coolidge	Battle of Bennington	New England	Grossular Garnet	French and Indian War
Painted Turtle	Ski (-ing)	Champlain Valley	Union	Lake Champlain

Vermont Bingo: Card No. 9

Vermont Bingo

Union	Maple	Burlington	River(s)	Executive Branch
Vermont Valley	Samuel de Champlain	Agricultural	Ethan Allan	Manufacture
Camel's Hump Mountain	Northern Leopard Frog		France	Climate
New England	Lake Champlain	Calvin Coolidge	Ski (-ing)	Green Mountain(s)
Champlain Valley	New Hampshire Grants	Judicial Branch	Seal	Northeast Highlands

Vermont Bingo

Chester Alan Arthur	Northern Leopard Frog	Rocks	Calvin Coolidge	New Hampshire Grants
Flag	Green Mountain(s)	Grossular Garnet	Insect(s)	Agricultural
Mount Mansfield	Manufacture		Judicial Branch	Hermit Thrush
Champlain Valley	Vermont Republic	Ski (-ing)	Camel's Hump Mountain	Union
Constitution	County (-ies)	Rutland	Border (-ed)	Covered Bridge(s)

Vermont Bingo

Covered Bridge(s)	Battle of Bennington	Green Mountain(s)	Maple	Insect(s)
Hermit Thrush	New Hampshire Grants	Apple(s)	Border (-ed)	Ethan Allan
Rutland	French and Indian War		Vermont Valley	River(s)
County (-ies)	Painted Turtle	Manufacture	Union	Mount Mansfield
Northern Leopard Frog	Flag	Camel's Hump Mountain	Constitution	Samuel de Champlain

Vermont Bingo

Calvin Coolidge	Battle of Bennington	Chester Alan Arthur	Green Mountain(s)	Vermont Valley
Apple(s)	Flag	Manufacture	Insect(s)	Climate
Maple	Samuel de Champlain		Hermit Thrush	French and Indian War
Northeast Highlands	Ski (-ing)	Burlington	Camel's Hump Mountain	Union
County (-ies)	Lake Champlain	Border (-ed)	Rutland	Grossular Garnet

Vermont Bingo: Card No. 13

Vermont Bingo

Fish	Manufacture	Rocks	Insect(s)	Constitution
Samuel de Champlain	Rutland	Green Mountain(s)	Ethan Allan	Northern Leopard Frog
Calvin Coolidge	France		Judicial Branch	Champlain Valley
Lake Champlain	Ski (-ing)	Camel's Hump Mountain	Burlington	Chester Alan Arthur
County (-ies)	River(s)	Climate	New Hampshire Grants	Northeast Highlands

Vermont Bingo

Grossular Garnet	Insect(s)	Rocks	Covered Bridge(s)	Maple
Chester Alan Arthur	Judicial Branch	Agricultural	Apple(s)	Constitution
Vermont Valley	Rutland		Vermont Republic	Northern Leopard Frog
County (-ies)	Green Mountain(s)	Flag	Ski (-ing)	Calvin Coolidge
New Hampshire Grants	Painted Turtle	Border (-ed)	Executive Branch	Hermit Thrush

Vermont Bingo

Burlington	Green Mountain(s)	Flag	Executive Branch	Red Clover
River(s)	Climate	French and Indian War	Mount Mansfield	France
Calvin Coolidge	Battle of Bennington		Vermont Valley	Hermit Thrush
Montpelier	Samuel de Champlain	County (-ies)	Grossular Garnet	Union
Constitution	"These Green Mountains"	Border (-ed)	Painted Turtle	Northern Leopard Frog

Vermont Bingo

Champlain Valley	Taconic Mountains	Legislative Branch	Green Mountain(s)	Fish
Grossular Garnet	Constitution	Ski (-ing)	France	French and Indian War
Insect(s)	Northeast Highlands		"These Green Mountains"	Flag
Lake Champlain	New Hampshire Grants	Union	Rocks	Climate
New England	Calvin Coolidge	Covered Bridge(s)	Maple	Battle of Bennington

Vermont Bingo: Card No. 17

Vermont Bingo

Executive Branch	Camel's Hump Mountain	Samuel de Champlain	Calvin Coolidge	River(s)
Northern Leopard Frog	Champlain Valley	New England	Vermont Valley	Constitution
Insect(s)	Climate		Legislative Branch	Apple(s)
Battle of Bennington	Agricultural	Ski (-ing)	Union	Judicial Branch
"These Green Mountains"	Green Mountain(s)	Rocks	Taconic Mountains	Chester Alan Arthur

Vermont Bingo

Vermont Valley	Chester Alan Arthur	Green Mountain(s)	Flag	Union
Grossular Garnet	Maple	Northern Leopard Frog	Covered Bridge(s)	France
Taconic Mountains	Camel's Hump Mountain		Ethan Allan	Vermont Republic
Judicial Branch	"These Green Mountains"	New England	Painted Turtle	Legislative Branch
Apple(s)	Red Clover	New Hampshire Grants	Northeast Highlands	Border (-ed)

Vermont Bingo

Fish	Taconic Mountains	Maple	Green Mountain(s)	Border (-ed)
Samuel de Champlain	Hermit Thrush	Mount Mansfield	New England	River(s)
Battle of Bennington	French and Indian War		Montpelier	Agricultural
Seal	Vermont Piedmont	Talc	Painted Turtle	"These Green Mountains"
Tribes	Northeast Highlands	Red Clover	Union	Legislative Branch

Vermont Bingo

Grossular Garnet	Chester Alan Arthur	Mount Mansfield	Green Mountain(s)	Seal
Battle of Bennington	Legislative Branch	Burlington	Flag	Rutland
Climate	New Hampshire Grants		Taconic Mountains	Rocks
New England	Covered Bridge(s)	"These Green Mountains"	Lake Champlain	Northeast Highlands
Montpelier	Red Clover	Border (-ed)	Champlain Valley	Painted Turtle

Vermont Bingo

Executive Branch	Judicial Branch	Legislative Branch	Apple(s)	Calvin Coolidge
River(s)	Maple	Vermont Republic	Flag	Ethan Allan
Samuel de Champlain	France		Rutland	French and Indian War
"These Green Mountains"	Lake Champlain	Painted Turtle	Agricultural	Mount Mansfield
Red Clover	Champlain Valley	Taconic Mountains	Climate	Montpelier

Vermont Bingo

Burlington	Taconic Mountains	Covered Bridge(s)	Apple(s)	Border (-ed)
Chester Alan Arthur	Fish	New Hampshire Grants	Grossular Garnet	Agricultural
Judicial Branch	Calvin Coolidge		Talc	Rutland
Climate	Red Clover	"These Green Mountains"	Champlain Valley	Painted Turtle
Seal	Vermont Piedmont	Northeast Highlands	New England	Legislative Branch

Vermont Bingo: Card No. 23

Vermont Bingo

Burlington	Northeast Highlands	Fish	Taconic Mountains	Flag
Legislative Branch	Border (-ed)	Mount Mansfield	River(s)	Rutland
French and Indian War	Executive Branch		Calvin Coolidge	Climate
Seal	Talc	"These Green Mountains"	Champlain Valley	Battle of Bennington
Tribes	Montpelier	Red Clover	Maple	Vermont Piedmont

Vermont Bingo

Montpelier	Mount Mansfield	Taconic Mountains	Rocks	Legislative Branch
Agricultural	Battle of Bennington	Grossular Garnet	Burlington	Ethan Allan
Lake Champlain	Flag		Talc	"These Green Mountains"
Vermont Republic	Seal	Vermont Piedmont	Red Clover	France
Border (-ed)	Fish	Samuel de Champlain	Constitution	Tribes

Vermont Bingo

Legislative Branch	Taconic Mountains	Judicial Branch	River(s)	Executive Branch
New England	Maple	Flag	Fish	Burlington
Lake Champlain	Talc		France	Montpelier
Champlain Valley	Apple(s)	Seal	Red Clover	"These Green Mountains"
French and Indian War	Constitution	Rocks	Vermont Piedmont	Tribes

Vermont Bingo

Judicial Branch	Samuel de Champlain	Taconic Mountains	Fish	Hermit Thrush
Seal	Talc	Grossular Garnet	"These Green Mountains"	Ethan Allan
Ski (-ing)	Vermont Piedmont		Red Clover	Montpelier
Executive Branch	Chester Alan Arthur	Mount Mansfield	Tribes	Agricultural
Constitution	France	Legislative Branch	Vermont Republic	French and Indian War

Vermont Bingo

Judicial Branch	Fish	Vermont Republic	Taconic Mountains	Burlington
Hermit Thrush	Legislative Branch	Talc	River(s)	France
Vermont Piedmont	Climate		French and Indian War	New England
Union	Executive Branch	New Hampshire Grants	Red Clover	"These Green Mountains"
Apple(s)	Insect(s)	Constitution	Tribes	Seal

Vermont Bingo: Card No. 28

Vermont Bingo

Legislative Branch	Fish	Executive Branch	Grossular Garnet	Insect(s)
Painted Turtle	New England	Mount Mansfield	French and Indian War	Vermont Republic
Lake Champlain	Talc		Ethan Allan	Taconic Mountains
Hermit Thrush	Seal	Manufacture	Red Clover	"These Green Mountains"
Burlington	Flag	Tribes	Chester Alan Arthur	Vermont Piedmont

Vermont Bingo

Camel's Hump Mountain	Taconic Mountains	River(s)	Insect(s)	"These Green Mountains"
Agricultural	Fish	Judicial Branch	France	Ethan Allan
Lake Champlain	Calvin Coolidge		French and Indian War	Mount Mansfield
Tribes	Chester Alan Arthur	Apple(s)	Red Clover	Talc
Seal	Vermont Valley	Vermont Piedmont	Legislative Branch	Vermont Republic

Vermont Bingo: Card No. 30

www.ingramcontent.com/pod-product-compliance
Lightning Source LLC
LaVergne TN
LVHW061339060426

835511LV00014B/2013